A Dorling Kindersley Book
Conceived, edited and designed by DK Direct Limited

Note to parents

What's Inside? Everyday Things is designed to help young children understand the way some familiar everyday things work. It shows how a refrigerator keeps food cold, what goes on behind a clock face, and how a camera and film together make photographs. It is a book for you and your child to read and talk about together, and to enjoy.

Editor   Hilary Hockman
Designers   Helen Spencer and Juliette Norsworthy
Typographic Designer   Nigel Coath

Illustrators   Paul Cooper and Jon Sayer
Photographers   Matthew Ward and Steve Tanner
Written by   Alexandra Parsons
Consultant   Helen Birch
Design Director   Ed Day
Editorial Director   Jonathan Reed

First published in Great Britain in 1992
by Dorling Kindersley Limited,
9 Henrietta Street, London WC2E 8PS

A CIP catalogue record for this book is available from the British Library.

ISBN 0-86318-986-5

Printed in Italy

WHAT'S INSIDE?

EVERYDAY THINGS

DK

DORLING KINDERSLEY
LONDON • NEW YORK • STUTTGART

TORCH

If you carry a torch, you carry light with you. A torch is very useful on camping holidays or if you are playing in the garden on a dark winter night. You often need one at home too, especially if you are looking for something in the back of a dark cupboard.

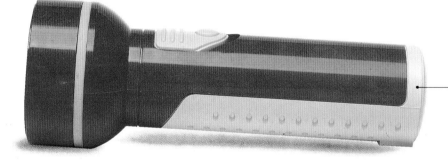

A torch is usually made of metal or tough plastic so it won't break if it is dropped.

You can see that the switch is on because all the metal strips are touching each other. Now electric power from the batteries can flow through to make the bulb glow.

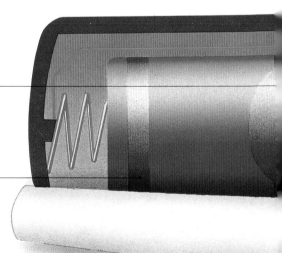

Batteries make electricity without wires and plugs! This torch needs two big batteries to make it work.

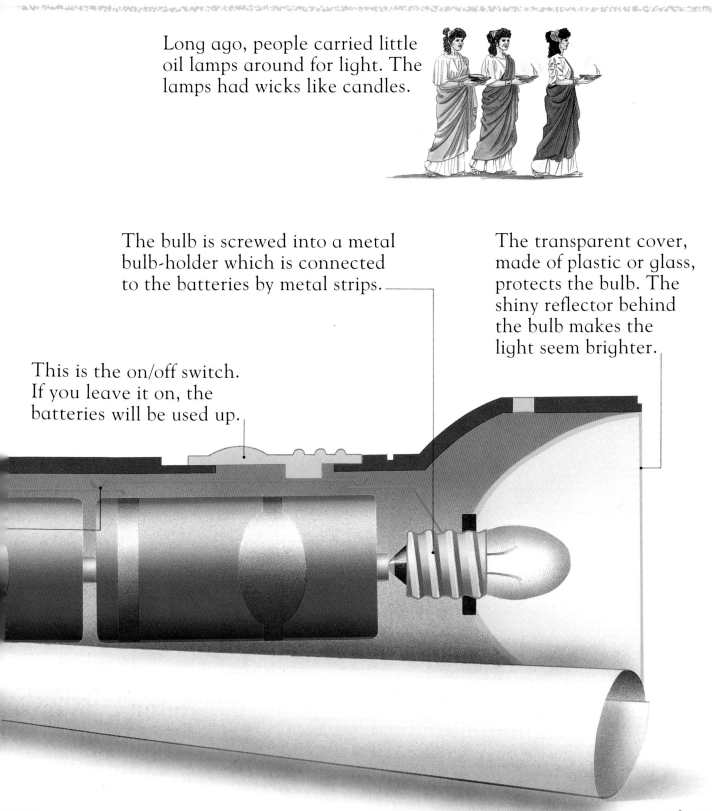

Long ago, people carried little oil lamps around for light. The lamps had wicks like candles.

The bulb is screwed into a metal bulb-holder which is connected to the batteries by metal strips.

The transparent cover, made of plastic or glass, protects the bulb. The shiny reflector behind the bulb makes the light seem brighter.

This is the on/off switch. If you leave it on, the batteries will be used up.

WASHING MACHINE

Thank goodness for washing machines! They take all the hard work out of washing clothes. To get clothes clean you have to push the soapy water through the clothes so the water will take the dirt away, and that's what a washing machine does.

The dials on the control panel are for setting water temperature, and washing and rinsing times. This load is going to need a long wash in hot water, but a pretty party dress may just need a quick, cool swish.

This washing machine has a lid on top where the clothes go in. Some have a door at the front.

Do you think this sock has been forgotten?

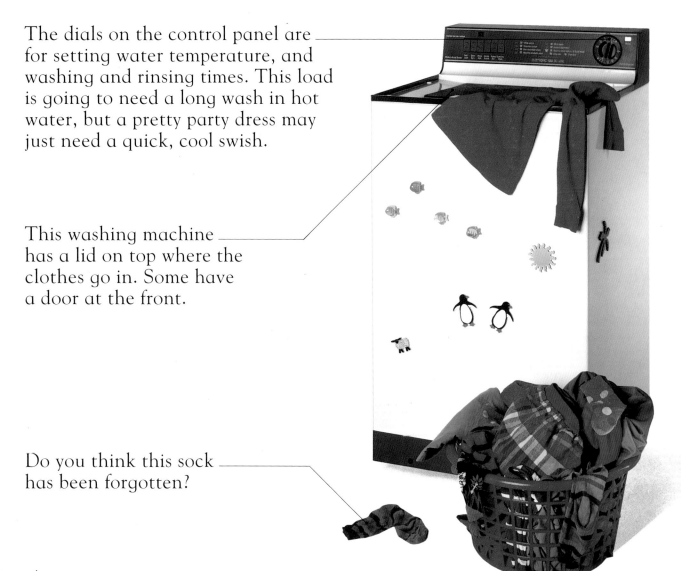

Early washing machines had to be filled from the pump, turned by hand and emptied with a hose pipe.

Clean water comes in through these pipes.

Dirty water comes out here. If the washing machine has done its job properly, the water will be dirty and the clothes will be clean!

This is the drum where the clothes are washed and rinsed. It has lots of holes in it so water can swirl in and out.

The paddle swishes the clothes from side to side.

The motor turns the drum round and round very fast at the end of the wash to spin all the rinsing water out.

STEAM IRON

Clothes come out of the washing machine crumpled and rumpled. Ironing them soon gets rid of all the creases and makes clothes look good and feel comfortable to wear.

This dial controls how hot the soleplate gets. The tougher the fabric, the hotter the iron needs to be. Delicate fabrics will burn or melt if the iron is too hot.

This is the soleplate. It is made of metal and gets very hot so don't touch!

The handle is made of special plastic that does not get hot.

Once upon a time...'smoothing irons', as they were called, were heated up on a charcoal fire, and ironing was a hot and dangerous business.

The water drips through this valve into the hot steam chamber where it is turned into steam.

Water is poured in here. It is turned into steam inside the iron and the steam comes out of little holes in the soleplate.

Steam comes out here to dampen the fabric.

The electric element heats the soleplate.

It is easier to press clothes smooth if they are damp.

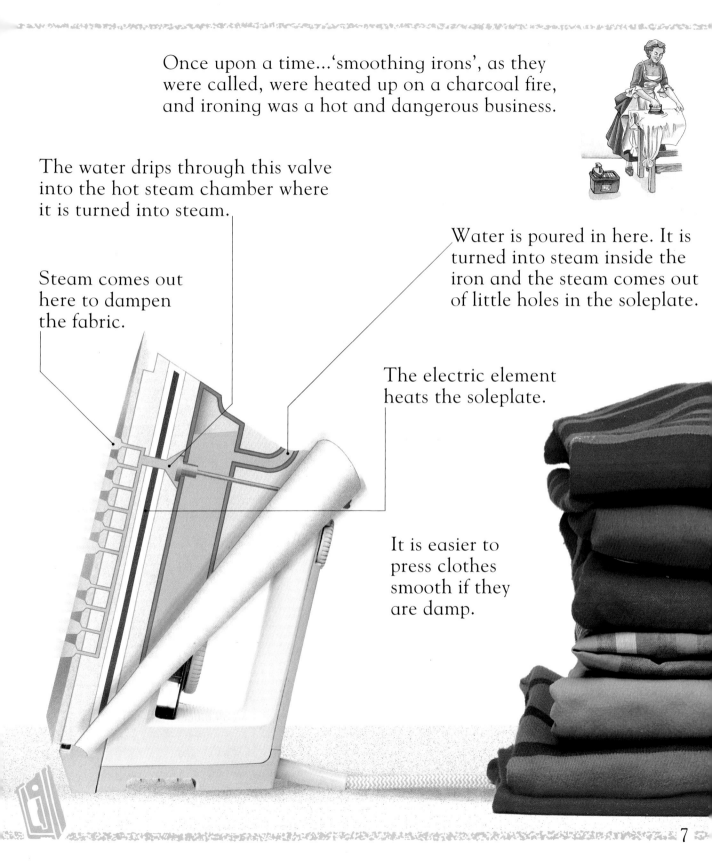

CLOCK

This is an alarm clock that works by clockwork. It doesn't need electricity or batteries. You just have to remember to wind it up every day. When you wind up a clock, you tighten a spring, and as the spring unwinds, it moves cog-wheels with little teeth which move the hands round and round.

This is the hammer that hits the alarm bells that make the noise that wakes you up in time to get to school.

Here's the big hand. The big hand takes one hour to go round the clock face...

You use this hand to set the alarm.

...and here's the little hand. It takes twelve hours to go round.

Once upon a time...people used to tell the time by looking at shadows cast by the sun. As long as the sun is shining, a sundial is very accurate, but of course it doesn't work at night and it hasn't got a bell!

This is the key that winds up the spring.

This lever sets off the alarm. It releases the hammer when the little hand reaches the time set on the dial. Don't forget to set the alarm before you go to sleep!

These are the cog-wheels that turn the hands of the clock.

As the spring unwinds it makes the cog-wheels go round.

CAMERA

To take a photograph, you need a camera. A camera takes in light just like your eyes do. The light that goes into a camera makes a picture on a layer of chemicals on a sheet of film. This picture stays hidden on the film until you take it to be developed and printed.

This little wheel winds the film round. When you've taken one picture, you wind on to a new piece of film to take another.

Click! When you press this button, you take a picture!

If you take a picture where there's not enough light, you must use the flash.

f/3.8 34mm

Sometimes your pictures aren't quite what you expected!

When cameras were just invented, it took a very long time for the light to make a picture on the film. People had to sit absolutely still for ten minutes or more.

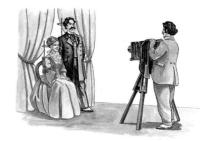

This is the shutter. When you press the button, its little sections spring open and shut again very quickly. It's like a tiny metal door.

This window is called the viewfinder. Through it you can see the picture you are going to take.

The film is stretched out across the back of the camera on rollers.

When the shutter opens, it lets light from the object in through this piece of thick glass called a lens. The light makes the picture on the film.

REFRIGERATOR

We keep fresh food in a cold fridge to stop the food going bad. Tiny invisible living things called bacteria are everywhere. If food is left lying around in warm air, the bacteria in it would grow and make the food go bad. Cold slows the growing bacteria down. Freezing stops them completely.

Can you think of foods that don't need to go in the fridge? Tinned foods like beans can be kept in a cupboard because no bacteria can get inside the tin – until you open it!

The freezer compartment is much colder than the rest of the fridge. In here, water turns to ice and fruit juice to ice lollies. Yum!

The inside of a fridge is covered with white plastic. It is easy to keep sparkling clean.

Close that door quickly! A fridge door has a rubber seal round it to make sure no cold air escapes and no warm air gets in.

Once upon a time...refrigerators were just cupboards filled with blocks of ice. They were designed like pieces of furniture.

Fridges cool food by taking warmth away from the air. Inside these pipes is a special liquid. As the liquid goes through the pipes, it turns into a gas and takes the heat away.

This part is called the condenser. It turns the gas back into a liquid.

As the gas turns to liquid again, it lets off the heat it has taken in. You can feel warm air coming from the grille at the front and now you know why!

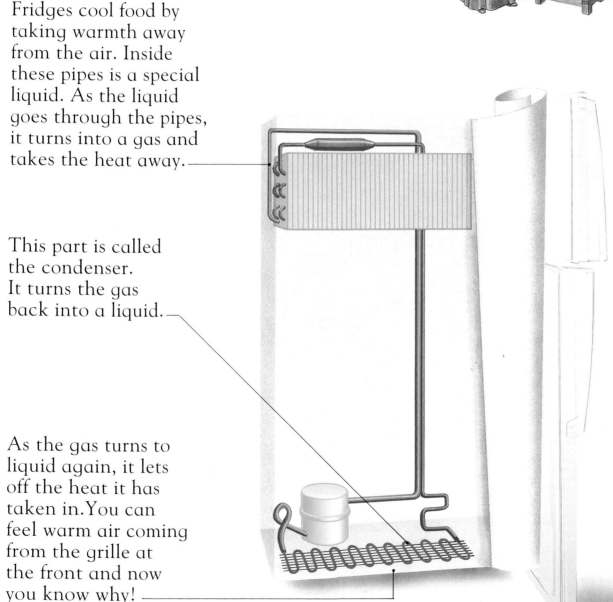

13

PERSONAL STEREO

On this small tape player you can listen to your favourite music
through earphones, without disturbing anyone else. Be careful
not to turn the volume too high – you could damage your ears!

This is where the earphones
plug in. The earphones are
like tiny loudspeakers.

Press the play
button to start
the music.

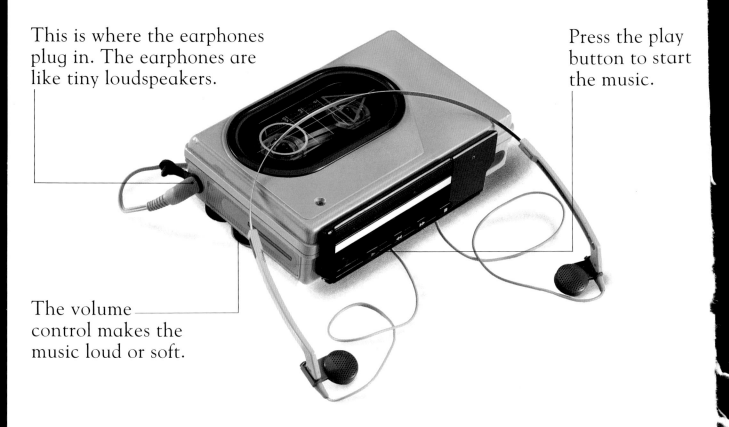

The volume
control makes the
music loud or soft.

Once upon a time...only kings,
queens and the nobility had
music wherever they went.

The drive motor turns a spindle that turns a little wheel in the centre of the tape spool. The wheel turns the tape round.

Inside the tape cassette, the tape winds from one reel to the other.

When the play button is pressed, this playing head moves forward to touch the tape. The tape passes its signal to the head.

Music for one side is recorded along the top of the tape, and for the other side, along the bottom.

The head passes the signal down the wires to the earphones so you can hear the music on the tape.

15

VACUUM CLEANER

Dust gets everywhere. It is floating about in the air all the time. It settles on carpets and furniture, making everything look grubby. This is where the vacuum cleaner comes in. A quick whizz round, and the house looks clean and fresh.

A vacuum cleaner works by sucking in dusty air. All you have to do is point the hose in the right place! The cleaning head is at the end of a long, bendy pipe.

The vacuum cleaner is on wheels so it can be pulled along easily.

This is the electric lead.

A vacuum cleaner will suck up everything that will go down the tube. Watch out for toys that haven't been put away!

Early vacuum cleaners needed two people to make them work. One person pumped the air, while the other used the hose to suck up dust.

The electric motor turns the fan.

The fan inside spins round so fast it pushes air out of the way, leaving a space with no air called a vacuum. Dusty air rushes up the bendy tube to fill the space.

The dusty air is sucked into this paper bag... with the toys. They nearly got lost forever! Air can go in and out of the bag. The dust and toys stay in the bag, but clean air comes out.

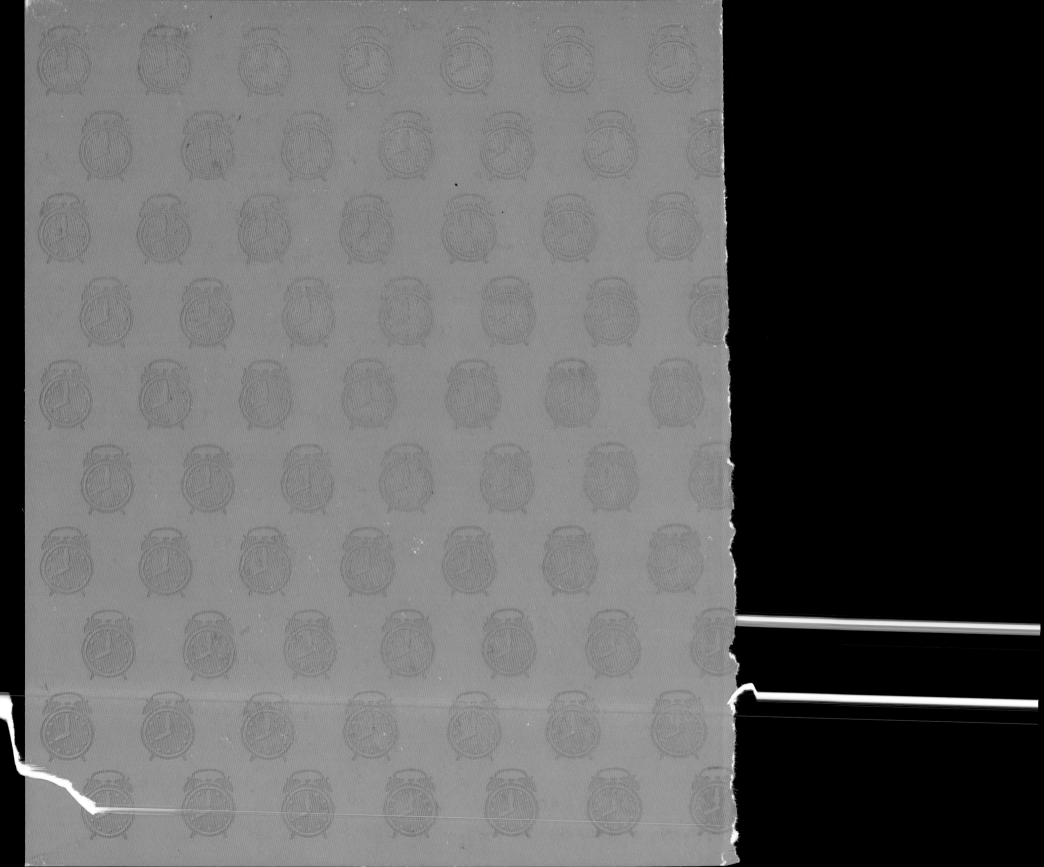